Jump, Little Wood Ducks

story by **Marion Dane Bauer**

photography by **Stan Tekiela**

Adventure Publications
Cambridge, Minnesota

Dedication

For Connor Dane Bauer, always!

–Marion Dane Bauer

To my darling Abby.

–Stan Tekiela

Cover photos by Stan Tekiela
All photos by Stan Tekiela except pg. 19 (dragonfly) and pp. 26–29,
used under license from Shutterstock.com

Story edited by Ryan Jacobson
Educational material edited by Sandy Livoti
Cover and book design by Jonathan Norberg

10 9 8 7 6 5 4 3 2 1

Jump, Little Wood Ducks

story by **Marion Dane Bauer**
photography by **Stan Tekiela**

Three little wood ducks alone in their nest, high in the hollow of a tree.

"Mama!" they cry. "Where's our mama? Where's our brothers and sisters?"

"Here we are," the brothers and sisters answer from way down at the bottom of the tree.

"Here I am," Mama answers from the bottom of the tree, too. "We're all down here waiting. Jump, little wood ducks."

The three remaining ducklings
look
down
and
down
and
down.

"Nope!" says duckling number one.

"No way, no how!" says the second duckling.

The last duckling just whispers, "Uh-uh."

"Jump, my strong ducklings," Mama says.
"Not so long ago, you were tucked inside an egg.
You poked and pecked, you pecked and poked
until you tumbled into your nest. Come tumble
into the world!"

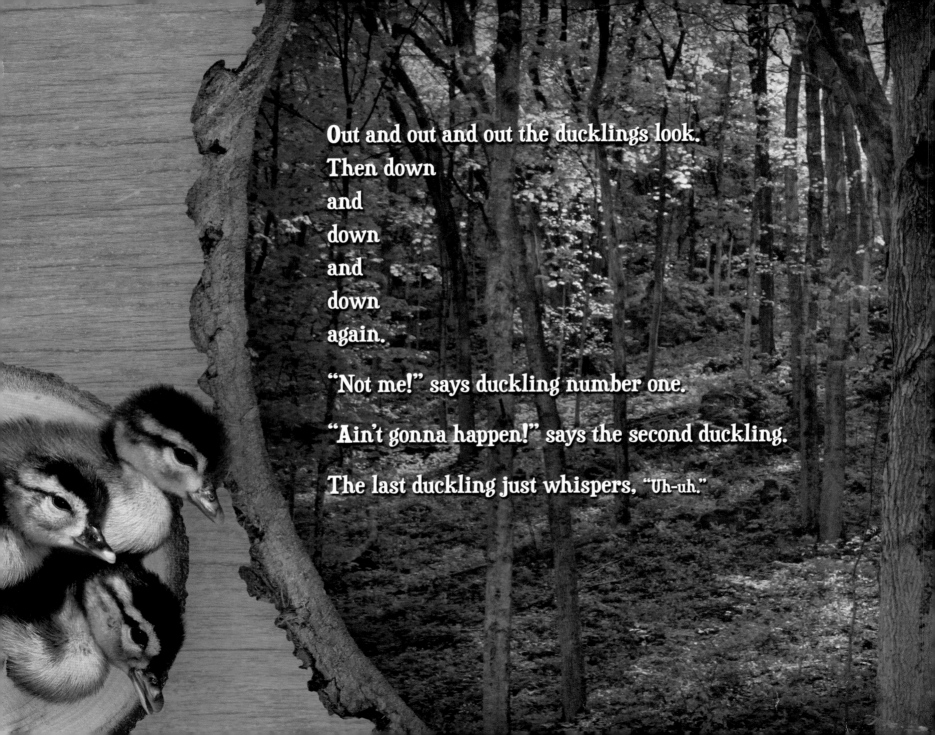

Out and out and out the ducklings look.
Then down
and
down
and
down
again.

"Not me!" says duckling number one.

"Ain't gonna happen!" says the second duckling.

The last duckling just whispers, "Uh-uh."

"Jump, my pretty ducklings," Mama says.
"See the trees, the flowers, the butterflies?
See your handsome papa on the pond?
Jump into the big, beautiful world."

"Our nest is beautiful," says duckling number one.
"And big, too."

"The world looks just fine from up here,"
says the second duckling.

The last duckling just whispers, "Uh-uh."

"Jump, my hungry ducklings," says Mama.
"Think about water bugs. Think water lilies, smartweed,
sweet flag. It's time for you to eat."

"Not so very hungry," says duckling number one.

"How about breakfast in bed?" says the second duckling.

The last duckling just whispers, "Uh-uh."

Mama walks back and forth, back and forth
at the bottom of the tree.
The brothers and sisters walk back and forth, too.

"If you don't jump," Mama says at last,
"you will never, ever, ever learn to fly."

"Who wants to do that?" cries duckling number one.

"Our wings are much too small," says the second duckling.

The last duckling just flaps those tiny wings and says,

"FLY! I'VE WANTED TO FLY SINCE I WAS AN EGG!"

"GO!" cries the last duckling, and the first duckling

jumps

from

the

nest.

"YOU, TOO!" she shouts, and the second duckling

follows.

The last duckling looks
down
and
down
and
down.

Then she . . .

...JUMPS!

And

falls

and

falls

and

falls.

She flaps her
baby wings.

Still

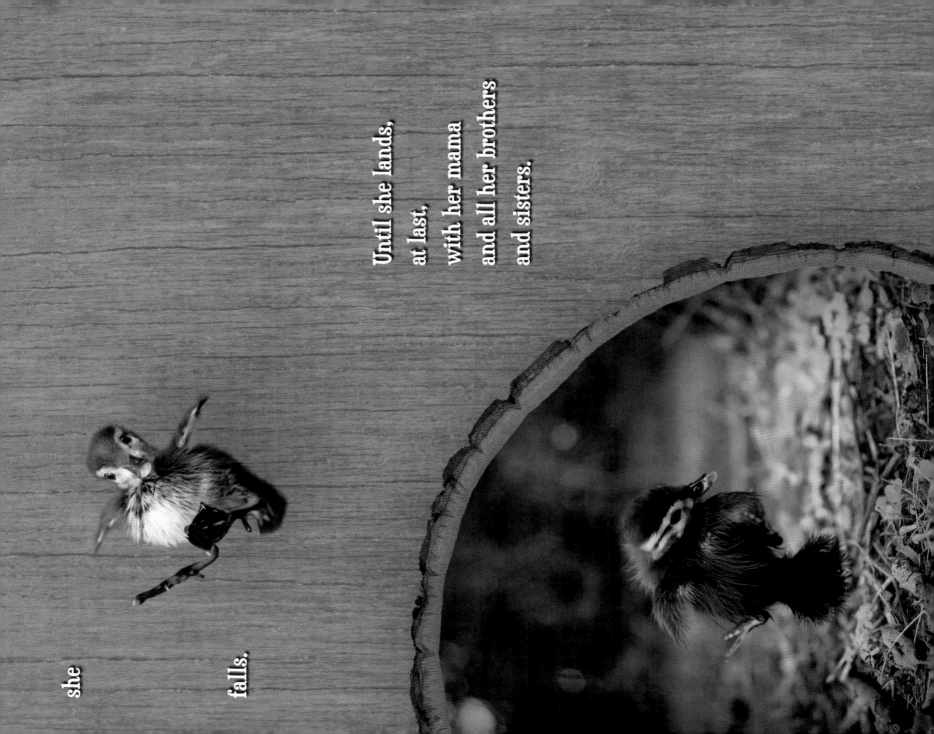

she

falls.

Until she lands,
at last,
with her mama
and all her brothers
and sisters.

"Wonderful, my dear ducklings!" says Mama. "Now let's go for a swim."

"Swim?" cries duckling number one.

"In the water?" asks the second duckling.

And the last duckling says . . .

"YOU MEAN YOU WANT US TO GET WET?"

Written by Stan Tekiela

What Are Ducks Doing in the Trees?

It seems a bit strange to see Wood Ducks nesting in tree cavities and perching or walking on branches, like songbirds. Truth is, other duck species also do these things—the Wood Duck is just the most common of tree ducks. Like ground-nesting ducks, they have webbed feet for paddling in water, but they also have extra long, sharp claws. Claws help Wood Ducks grip and maneuver around the tree branches.

Wood Ducks Are Safe High Up

Wood Ducks are cavity-nesting waterfowl. They use existing tree cavities for nesting, or wooden nest boxes made by people. Nesting in a cavity is a good way to avoid ground-dwelling predators that eat eggs. It also protects them from harsh springtime weather.

Mama Duck Chooses the Best Place to Nest

Female Wood Ducks choose the nest site and often return to the same tree for several years. Most nests are about 30 feet above the ground, but some are more than 100 feet high! While Wood Ducks prefer cavities in trees near water, many nests are over a mile away from water—which means those mothers and babies have a long walk after they leave the nest.

Flying Through the Forest

Wood Ducks have shorter, broader wings than other ducks, which help them to fly in branch-filled forests. Their shorter wings allow them to slip through tight openings in the trees' branchy canopy. They fly at high speeds through the woods, traveling to and from the nest cavity.

Security in the Male Wood Duck's Presence

The male stays near the female to protect her while she selects the nest site and lays eggs. She lays upwards of 15 eggs and incubates them for just over a month, but once she starts laying eggs, the male leaves and joins other males in the area. The female raises the ducklings on her own.

Do Wood Duck Babies Really Jump from Their Nests?

Within 24 to 48 hours of hatching, the ducklings are eager to jump out of the nest and get started in life. Before leaving the nest, the mother allows her ducklings to climb and jump all over her. Mama sits patiently while the youngsters jump around like popcorn popping. She doesn't help the babies jump—they do it all on their own.

When the mother decides it's time to leave, she flies to the ground and calls softly to the ducklings. Each duckling climbs swiftly to the cavity entrance and launches into the air. They jump one at a time or go out 2 or 3 together. The entire process of leaving the nest takes under 2 minutes. All ducklings need to exit quickly so that the whole group can stay together with their mother.

How Safe Is It to Jump from High Up?

The newly hatched ducklings are small and weigh next to nothing, so when they hit the ground they don't get hurt. They lack the body weight (mass) to land with enough force to injure themselves. Instead, they bounce like rubber balls and quickly follow their mother away from the cavity tree.

Good Food in the Water and on Land

A water environment helps to protect ducks from land-dwelling predators, and baby Wood Ducks don't need coaxing to get there. They take to water instinctively, just like adult ducks.

Once in the water, ducklings learn what to eat by trial and error. This natural feeding behavior is common in all duck species. As ducklings, Wood Ducks feed heavily on the teeming aquatic insects in shallow ponds and streams. When they become adults, they switch their main diet to plants and seeds, favoring acorns and maple seeds.

More Gee-Whiz Facts About Wood Ducks

Wood Duck males are considered by many to be the most beautiful duck in North America. They are multicolored with some iridescent plumage and distinctive red eyes.

Wood Ducks are among the few duck species that can be attracted to nest in your yard. Simply put up a Wood Duck nest box! Females will lay eggs in the nests of neighboring females. This "egg dumping" results in excess of 20 eggs in some clutches.

In the wild, the average Wood Duck lives only 3 to 5 years. They are highly migratory in the northern part of their range, but they don't migrate in the southern areas.

Wood Ducks were nearly hunted into extinction in the early 1900s. They are doing much better now, with stable populations all over the country.

About the Author

Marion Dane Bauer is the author of more than 100 books for young people, ranging from novelty and picture books to early readers, both fiction and nonfiction, books on writing, and middle-grade and young-adult novels. She has won numerous awards, including the Minnesota Book Award, a Jane Addams Peace Association Award for her novel *Rain of Fire*, an American Library Association Newbery Honor Award for her novel *On My Honor* and the Kerlan Award from the University of Minnesota for the body of her work. Her books have been translated into more than a dozen languages. She was one of the founding faculty and the First Faculty Chair of the country's first Master of Fine Arts in Writing for Children and Young Adults at Vermont College of Fine Arts. She continues today to teach through her blog at www.mariondanebauer.com.

About the Photographer

Naturalist, wildlife photographer and writer Stan Tekiela is the author of the popular Wildlife Appreciation book series that includes *Backyard Birds*. He has authored more than 165 field guides, nature books, children's books, wildlife audio CDs, playing cards and other products, presenting many species of birds, mammals, reptiles, amphibians, trees, wildflowers and cacti in the United States. With a Bachelor of Science degree in Natural History from the University of Minnesota and as an active professional naturalist for more than 25 years, Stan studies and photographs wildlife throughout the United States and Canada. He has received various national and regional awards for his books and photographs. Also a well-known columnist and radio personality, his syndicated column appears in more than 25 newspapers and his wildlife programs are broadcast on a number of Midwest radio stations. Stan can be followed on Facebook and Twitter. He can be contacted via www.naturesmart.com.

Get the First Three Children's Books from the Award-Winning Duo

You'll love all the titles that pair Marion Dane Bauer's touching stories with Stan Tekiela's incredible photography. All three books are award winners, including *Baby Bear Discovers the World*, which won the 2007 Mom's Choice Award for Most Outstanding Children's Book.